The Taj Express

L|M

Also by Alan Ross
Poetry
Poems 1942–67

Travel
Time Was Away (with John Minton)
The Gulf of Pleasure
The Bandit on the Billiard Table

Cricket
Australia 55
Cape Summer
Through the Caribbean
Australia 63
West Indies at Lords

General
The Forties

ALAN ROSS

The Taj Express

Poems 1967-73

LONDON MAGAZINE EDITIONS
1973

© Alan Ross, 1973

SBN 900626 83 6

Published by London Magazine Editions
30 Thurloe Place, London S.W.7

Printed in Great Britain by
Billing & Sons Limited, Guildford and London

Contents

Part I

Along the Neva

These palaces staining the Neva,
Splintering under keels of launches,
Become rainbows of soft glass,
Winter thawed out of them—
And cruising the old hideouts
Smeared with memory and mist,
One marvels at such visions,
Their enduring fragility.

Yet solid and indestructible,
A chance gift bestowed on these formidably
Plain and essential people, incongruously
Stepping on carpets of autumn,
As if they should wipe their feet
Before such resplendent domes the colour of sun.

Navy Museum, Leningrad

Marooned by a downpour we stare
Hour after hour at stills of Soviet epics,
Blown-up and grainy. They are already historic,
These revolutionary encounters, where, smelling like fur
Of wet animals, today's crews take refuge too.
The Soviet Union loves Heroes and huge here
They fire guns or reduced to toys
Give scale to models. It's a Boys
Own Exhibition where everything is true,
Neither enemies nor Allies obscuring the view.

Mooning from picture to picture, these curious
Men, noses to canvas, follow me, the furious
Rain pitting the Neva. They exhale gloom,
Faces like rind of bacon. I assume
Their expression of awe, noticing my own ship,
Wrongly captioned, trailing its carcass
Towards Kola. Perhaps it's a slip.
History has always been subject to bias,
And here what's important is giving a bloom
To sacrifice, ideas a high gloss
Regardless of accuracy. This temple to sailors
Of a fleet more mutinous than deadly sprays
Nostalgia like musk, records no failures.

Revolution Anniversary

I dream something knocking in my skull,
Only this hammering's outside. A full
Moon turns old scaffolding blue. All
Is being prepared for celebration, every wall
Lacquered, leaves swept as they fall.

A faint hangover, a faintly sour taste
Predictable after such junketing, such feasts
Of vodka. I stumble in false haste
For the alkaseltzer, reluctant to waste
Any of the morning, its revelatory yeast.

A zoo-like reverberation from the corridor,
The guardian crone established on each floor
To prevent orgy. Snore after snore,
Until gradually the door
Assumes colour and handle, and the poor
Wretch humps bedclothes and dreams into store.

Approaching Kronstadt

Smudges of grey on the brown Baltic,
The stone islands come at us, septic
And marshy. And I experience that familiar
Sinking of the spirit, as if treachery
And confinement had smells of their own,
Borne by the harsh syllables of Kronstadt.

Last night we entered the Gulf of Finland,
Coasts snowfree and coniferous, barely recognisable
As that unsmiling promontory, iced-in and sable,
We once slid up on with aircraft and curses.
In the bar, high on cheap vodka, Trade Unionists
Sang the Red Flag, danced if they were able.

Ahead of us a fleet rots in its lair,
Captive of itself, but wrapped in the air
Of an old secretiveness, faith in the protective
Mysteries like a charm on it. Spectral
And anonymous, without clues to identity,
Ships brood in collusion, dissembling as fakes.

On a breeze of ambergris and mud gulls break
From a flat estuary and now, in our herringbone wake,
The batteries disperse. Standing on deck
With my son, half my age then, I pass him
The binoculars that brought into live focus
Those names Sverdlov, Odessa, that seem suddenly shrunk.

We enter the canal, rain like soot
Falling. He turns up his windcheater, lapels
A cluster of badges, profiles of cosmonaut,
Lenin, gleaming on damp serge. And precariously seated
On damp railings, binoculars raised, his fragility conveys
The real sense of a circle completed.

Night Porter

Perusing his Form Book in a glass booth,
Around him the familiar hum of generators,
A lift creaking like stores from the hold,
The smell of tea in sickly confinement,
He might be back in his reeking messdeck,
Never seeing daylight, on edge with ulcers.

With a kind of regret for the old days,
The slavish stink of condensed milk
And seaboots, the steeplechasing cockroaches;
When, among cronies, he surveyed an empire
Slung between stars and a sliding ocean
As softly sustaining as a silken pavilion.

Iceland at the Bottom of a Glass

Swirling angostura over ice
I watch the furred suns fill
The whole window with light
—snow on the Downs packed tight—
The ice in my glass slice
Into shapes, fjord into fjord spill.

It is the same cleft
And glacial view, as looking back
On the rim of the Arctic
I once saw Vatnojökull melt as we left,
Peaks streaked this aromatic
Bittersweet pink, flushing sea irretrievably black.

Stocking Shop, Seydis Fjord, 1942

Standing on a ladder
Stretching for the top shelf, she'd swivel suddenly
And remark they were out of them,
Surprising the matelots craning their necks,
Her own rolled stocking-tops nipping plump thighs
Like the lips of balloons.

It was an old trick, often repeated,
But for a long time they fell for it,
Starved of stockings and silkiness,
And when she bid them come back
At the last moment before sailing,
They could never resist it,
Going to their graves with torpedoes of nylon.

Station Hotel

Under the smoked domes
Of giant glasshouses the rails
Seem extensions of legs,
The window an arch through which
Everything travels. Her bruises
Lie like soot on orchids, the room
Echoing departure, steamy with arrival.

Where, despite shunting
Of engines, a murderous air
Of the conservatory drifts
As if fresh from the forest,
And windows like sky through fernleaves
Glint above expresses
That alight on buffers gently as butterflies.

Palace of Culture, Sinaia

In former days plump blondes,
Stepping from iced furs, tightened their buttocks
On the hands of drunk courtiers. Glass crashed.
Snow was a kind of madness
Mixed with blood and spilled vodka, harsh cries
Of officers on horseback. Swords glinted
In moonlight curdled on blue rivers,
Pines and birch upright as guardsmen.

A palace famed for debauchery,
Where sailors fresh from the Caspian
Roughed up the bodies of dancers.
Now the rococo and mirrored ceilings,
Oceans of nudity, record hairdos
Of secretaries, typing in triplicate—
Partings like fishbones, thighs
Woollenly adhesive. In this museum,

Dedicated to detaching from the past
Its splendour, conformism has its deserts,
Ballrooms waltzing to railwaymen, the woodpecker
Clatter of compositors, writers
Like battery-hens laying in captivity. In Sinaia
Effort is rewarded, contact with corruption
A trophy for the enslaved, their tributes exacted.
Under these onion domes culture is obedience.

Mammaia

A gimcrack resort for 'the workers',
Where behind cracked palings
Huge women are segregated,
Naked in excess like beached seals,
Oiled and disposable.

Everything is over life-size,
Breasts and bottoms gigantic as hoardings,
A great come-on for industry.
And their comrades from the union,
Eyes to holes in the paling,
Look rapt as men at microscopes
Or gunsights, trigger-happy.

The beach is crowded as a supermarket,
The sea is dishcloth grey.
Heads float in groups like tealeaves
And concrete hotels rise to a uniform height.
In the hills are painted Moldavian churches.

A Card from the Café Pierre Loti

High over the Horn
Mosques and factories spectral on water
The same tables set among pines
The same sunsets reviving as alcohol
The smell of charcoal and mint tea
And towards Ismir the same steamers
Bringing the East nearer

Which already inhabited him,
This Turk by adoption, in high collar
And tarboosh, moustaches askew,
Luckier than most of us
To have acquired so exotic a view
From his own fantasies, reclining among silk
Cushions, hookah at his elbow.

You can see him happily
Dolled up on the back of this postcard,
Host to an evening of imperial twilight,
The books no longer read, the dark
Falling on him, as on this muddle
Of domes and smokestacks, the East's
Voluptuous visions reduced to images
Of riot and earthquake. Still, the pages
Have a curious scent, improbably haunting.

Trial at Amalfi

In the Chiostro del Paradiso
Palm trees are like rooks' wings at rest
Or folded umbrellas. Black has come
To sit in judgment, the musty
Gowns of lawyers, dusty cassocks.

It is surprising
In the city of Flavio Goia,
Inventor of the compass,
To come on this gravely maritime
Mourning, shadows damp as seaweed,
And the heat only hindrance
For those going about their business,
Concerned with duty, the dispensing of justice.

Summer belongs here, the white
Arrows of steamers ripping the blue,
Wagner at Ravello deep in Parsifal,
And the season running out like a streamer
Thrown among fireworks and trodden . . .
All the same, in these cloisters,
Thanks to Goia and others, we can prepare
For voyages of one kind or another,
Priests in their rust robes
Specific in their tasks as sailors, though as vague
About itineraries, the motives for travelling.

On the Bosphorus

Below my balcony a swarthy contralto,
Her face like a sweetmeat,
Coarse hair and secret emulsions,
Soaps at her bosom. She juggles it,
Warbling Aïda. Often at night
I watch her embracing the moon,
Shuffling her roof in see-through nightdress.

She distracts me, as now
Do two teams of birds, come upon
One another as if by chance,
Who toss her drawers as they dry
In some kind of aerial tennis,
Worrying the mauve satin
With the same exaggerated persistence dogs
And lawyers affect when odours resist them.

Moscow—Delhi

It is 1 a.m., the transit lounge
Freezing. I open *Anna Karenina*
'Happy families are all alike; every
Unhappy family is unhappy
In its own way' but cannot,
Under the gaze of Lenin,
Vast blow-ups of dams and collectives,
Settle to it. My fellow passengers,
Pakistani and Indian, drained of their colour,
Whisper through striped mufflers.

I am going home, if home
Is where you come from. I imagine
The thin rind of orange
That over the Himalayas will mean dawn
And Delhi, drums and desertion.
Half my life ago, in this same snow,
Smelling this same smell of sour bread
And cabbages, I left Russia,
Unhappy in my own way, more eager still for take-off.

Part II

Airgraphs from West Indies

Caroni

Sometimes at dusk
Returning through lanes heady with hibiscus
We come across groups of cricketers,
Indians mostly, and visible
As blurs of flannel, their high laughs
Skimming the river like silver.

Around us the ibis,
Wounded by sunset, take off
In flocks of vermilion. We pass
Lines of women in saris, melting
Like the sky into velvet. Dogs howl,
And past village stalls
Smells of rum and roti hang on us still.

Mongoose

Half-squirrel, half-rat, but with the incisors
Of the real killer, he has come
Into his own silk empire. In naves
Of cool cane he basks like a voluptuary,
Savouring his whiskers. He is in charge now,
Wet-mouthed addict from whom, like the cutters,
Africa is remote, a mere rolling of eyes.
They have won through together,
Shedding their serfdom. Thus do we see them,
Plush overseers on the crown of the road,
Those nights when we cruise through molasses,
Our headlamps spraying long grasses
That sometimes are set fire to. Homeless,
Then, these rodent police, eyes like paraffin,
Scuttle before us, their empire in flames.

Diamond Rock

Adieu, Foulard, adieu, Madras

Behind us in a collar of cloud
Morne Rouge, the bay liverish,
And up through Trois-Islets,
La Pagerie, tree-ferns like airships,
To this ruin of a village,

A bottle of white rum called Josephine,
Fish soup and drains
A child with coal eyes squatting.

And sometimes hidden from us
Diamant coming in and out of the rain
An island like a bowler hat
Bluejackets caught in its brim.

Lost empires, lost chances,
A woman among mangroves
Shedding her bikini,
And hard off canoes the throb
Of sun and creole music.

Mayaro

Between Manzanilla and Mayaro
The beach runs straight as a ruler.
You can drive a car on it.
The Atlantic comes in on foam curlers,
And between them and the crocodile river
Royal palms are as splendid as Nubians.

We have hauled up hundreds
Of chip-chips, silvery bivalves the sun polishes.
All morning we swam among Indians on bicycles,
Lying out in the shade of a hotel
Going bankrupt. The forest encroaches,
Tying up balconies with festooning liana.

In Port of Spain

On the savannah are twenty-six cricket pitches,
The Hilton overlooks them and Government House also.
Racehorses are ridden out on pearly mornings,
Spacing their droppings under shapely flame trees.
Athletes and others are well catered for,
Though the sea attracts only foreigners. Nevertheless,
For all these recreational facilities,
Life doesn't exist in a vacuum, and the vacuum
Sometimes hits you like the first suck of a hurricane.

Driving through St Lucia

Striped banana-buses of St Lucia.

Dashboards strewn with fern and rosaries
They bear on their sides propitiatory names
Forever my Love
Northern Angel
Patience
Prayer
All Over.

Red, canary, cobalt, these pullmans
Of the poor on cricket days become
Pavilions in forest clearings.

From Marigot to Anse de Sables their green loads
Slither and slide as we pass them, the Pitons
Soft as mauve wool, the Atlantic blue lint.

Impoverished by separation, lovelorn,
Like them we need to propitiate.

Choiseul, Souffrière, and, at last, Vieux Fort,
Shirts stuck to our backs, bones aching.
In the high passes amongst mango and breadfruit
Immortelles shaded us like rusty umbrellas.

The sea, shanty-lined, has the glitter of tinfoil.
In it we taste, touch, shed everything,
In blue embraces become simple as fishes.

Part III

Part III

The Gateway of India

The first addictive smell
And that curiously sated light
In which dhows and islands float
Lining the air with spices.

The beginning and end
Of India, birth and death,
The bay curved as a kukri
And on Malabar Hill the vultures,
Like seedy waiters, scooping the crumbs off corpses.

South of Madras

At Mahalibaripuram
There is only the temple
A dead cobra draped on the rocks like a belt
The man having his hair cut
Three women in saris.

The beach runs for ever,
Salt spraying the pagodas,
The lion, the bull and the elephant
Halted in their tracks,
And the stone chariots hub-deep in sand.
The Pallava empire ended here,
Where Durga and the buffalo wrestled
And the hoofmarks of a horse
Cantering along wet sand contract
And expand like the valves of a heart

Bengal

Against the betel-stained violence
The senseless murders that appal
The oppression of words and climate
That breathe Bengal

You must set the softness of heart,
A querulous literacy,
And the old ox-eyed gentleness
That rips them apart.

Rush-hour, Calcutta

'The hour of the cowbells' is what
These sometimes abstemious Bengalis,
Camped in their homeless dusk

Call that delirious moment
When light melts and car-horns mellow,
And we in our whisky culture

Fret in the traffic, smoke
From the jute mills coating the Hooghly,
Faces like pebbles bleaching the maidan.

It is the moment when saris
And soft drinks, sweetmeats and sweet eyes,
Take on the colour of sunset,

Expresses hooting out of Howrah,
Tent-flaps opening like mouths.

The Swimmer, Udaipur

Daily at noon the solitary swimmer
Measures his distance to Jag Nivas,
Island of parrots and palace ruins.
His oiled topknot slits the lake
Like a periscope or bird's crest.
Blurred eyelids dissolve to houseboats,
Open to hills and smoke-gold temples,
And on the way back the reverse.
This obsessive curving of one arm
After the other through brown water
Is an act of love and penance.
Pink saris are music to him.
He wades out past masseurs and dhobis
Reducing flesh and cloth to essentials,
Waste like colour seeping from linen . . .
At dusk, sometimes, sadness like smoke
Or mist veils the islands, there is the sound
Of sitars, voices that fall or wail.

Erotic Sculptures at Khajuraho

After the long night
Close to each other, their profound
But simple needs met by their mouths
Skilled in such loving, they awoke
To bulbuls tinny as bangles
Sky sliced watermelon.

And taking off
On the long flight to Khajuraho,
Ox eyes like sidelights on runways,
Hills of dried blood,
They still tasted each other,
Felt sky like blue in their veins.

Only at the temples,
Places of greenness and great movement,
Where love was elaborated like chess,
The instinctual given a number,
Did ideas of religion drop from them,
Like sleep from eyelids, sun shut by an umbrella.

Half-caste

Haunted by India,
That girl gazing at her belly
In the bathroom mirror,
I imagine her long thighs
The colour of storks among rice fields,
Mauve anemones, waterwheels . . .

It is a particular
Narcissism of the half-caste,
Jewelled navel, the neck inquiring
In that familiar defensiveness
Of arrogance or insult. The voice yields,
And, surfacing, I remember
Breasts flat in my eyes like waterlilies,
Her hands where water reached.

The Grove of the Perfect Being

Handsome as Shashi Kapoor,
Idol of the Indian cinema, he is perfectly
Turned out—flowered shirt,
Wide belt, white suit, buckle shoes,
Silvery as a fish with chains and bracelets—
And aware of having a way
With him, though not my way.
He is the self-appointed guide
And impresario to 'the Grove
Of the Perfect Being', at one
With the past and the place,
Site among the mangos of the earliest
Of Bhubaneswar's many temples.

Son of a priest of a priest,
He assumes the right to whatever perks
Are going; he'd rather
It were a cinema or garage,
But there it is. The patter
Has become second nature,
Kalinga and Asoka, Durga
And Hanuman, the Monkey God,
Rajani and Lingaraj,
More boring than chat about torques
And facias, discbrakes or suspension,
But—with luck—good for some baksheesh.
And leaping in front of us,
Brushing aside our mild demurrings,
He swings his transistor, repeating
Parrot-fashion a lengthy rigmarole
As apparently incomprehensible
To himself as to others,
Flashing a smile like a grand piano.

When it is all over
And 'The Golden Age of temple building'

With its *shikharas* and *toranos*,
Jagamohans and *bhogmandirs*,
Has been confused beyond recognition,
He discourses on the Lord Siva
And his lingam, on Parvati
And the *mithuna* couples whose antics
Are obviously more to his own liking.

And at last allowing us
Actually to enter a temple,
With a sly smirk points to elephants
And what he calls 'cocrodiles',
Cobras and hermits and dancing girls,
Dwarfs and lions. 'In this one
The cocrodile is entering the water,
And in this one the lady
Is being entered from behind,
One of the popular positions
Favourable for penetration.'

He is pleased with his joke,
Slipped as silkily in as only
Long practice can manage,
And he awaits our reaction,
A bit down for a second,
But soon back in top gear,
Drawing our attention
To what scarcely needed it,
Endless friezes of copulation,
Men and women their legs round each other,
Priests and prostitutes,
The holy and the wholly pleasurable.

At Bhubaneswar there is plenty
Of both, and leaving the Bundu Sagar
'The sacred lake' it is possible
To reflect on the sad separateness

Of our Christian culture,
Puritanism the alternative
To exploitation on the crudest
Of levels. Even here
In this mango-grove of temples,
Nothing is allowed to be
What it was, the exchange
Of favours for their own sake,
Two bodies making what they can
Of momentary ecstasies, before
The curtains come down, the showmen appear.

A Grandmother in Calcutta

It was always afternoon
When we went there, everything in shade,
The palms like splayed umbrellas, the frayed
Banana leaves the same colour
As the bead curtains rattling on the verandah,
My grandmother rocking back and forth.

Huge and handsome, she seemed
Physically as rooted as indeed she was
By birth and tradition, growing
Out of the floorboards like a vast lettuce
Gone to seed, but entirely there
In her frail finery, about her a kind of glowing

Nostalgia that bred images
Of eminence, in which she washed us
As if they were a stream still flowing
—French planters of indigo, Irish colonels dead early
Of drink or dysentry, East Indiamen, judges,
Directors of jute mills, surgeons, burly

Impresarios of the railway, moustaches
Venomous but with a family stutter.
Now at last they had run out, too many
Killed too young, and what flowed
Or flowered were the stains and gashes,
Dry rot in the floorboards where Granny

Pat rocked under the insults of mynahs,
One loopy daughter puffing from a green holder,
Banging out preludes on a tinny piano,
The other, a saint in her way, never back
From tending the backward, and always the smell
Of bananas and cigarettes, poverty growing bolder.

Coco de Mer

White schooners of Port Galud
White sand of Praslin
In the vallée de mai green appropriates
Nuts with secretions of love milk
Nuts soft-grained as turtles

The goddess spreads her legs
Vulva as icon yoni as icon
And these coco de mer
Washed up from Mahé,
Polished by the long haul
Of ocean, are become
Objects of worship, ritual
Adornments with sea-taste of women.

A Wartime Present

A map of India carved,
As it might be a heart, on the back
Of a cigarette case. In uniform pockets
I could trace the shape of Bengal,
Calcutta alive at my fingertips,
The Hooghly through ice. On deck
After dinner, nights mild or atrocious,
I'd inhale childhood—drifts
From the compound of curry and *pan*,
Smells of the racecourse, betel-stains
Like blood in the speech of bearers—
All that remained to set against drowning,
Tall seas turned on their backs
Like doped tigers, allegiances of the exile
Without family, without family feeling.

The boundaries became wrong, ghosts
Of a forfeited unity, but their fading
Disguised it. The rub of materials,
Naval serge, flannel, white duck,
Had worn out the heart, the old essences
Thinned into nothing. And the case,
Lying in a drawer for years, had lost
Its suggestiveness. Only now,
Coming on it suddenly and carrying it
Back to Bengal, do I feel
Under my fingers like braille
The frontiers begin to come true,
The heart beat from the gold. I take
The case from my pocket and here,
In Calcutta, open it to the air,
Hoping that more will adhere
Than the stew of corpses and cowdung—
Something of the old power to evoke
Images that might last out a life.

Fishing Boats off Puri

Amazing that these mere
Ideas of boats, three scooped trunks
Of ilex tied together, and peppery sails
The texture of rice paper

Should charm such vast breakers,
Cyclonic gales combing a nervy
Bengal sea, its platter
Of stubborn fish like votive offerings
Flat as pewter, worn down by water.

Yogis at Chowpatty Beach

Only their heads are visible
As if decapitated, or on cocktail sticks,
Bodies in coffins of sand, beards floating.
It is a way of detachment. Bhelpuri stalls,
Their awnings striping the beach
Like bathing huts, do not disturb them.
They are immune to the smells of spices.

The ocean is bronze, the horses
And cows plodding its edge, black.
Tonight, sunset has silenced politics,
There are no speakers
In the shadow of Tilak, stone orator,
No cries of corruption, fist-shakings.

Instead, the dynamic of silence,
Vertical yellow disposed
By saddhus. On Tilak
Marigold wreaths are bruised to saffron.
And, hoisting their dhotis,
Clerks open umbrellas as insurance,
Wading to a backcloth of dhows,
The Arabian sea under surveillance.

In Cochin

On the verandah, at the water's edge,

A dark man in a white suit,
Pink gin, and an airmail *Times*

Or a white man in a dark suit
Reading the *Cochin Gazette*,

Depending on the day or the light.

He is without identity,
A fingerprint on a door, or shape in a cane chair

Like myself, watching the fishing nets
Strain sunset through mesh claws.

The cemetery is full of our ancestors.
On a torn cloth we play snooker,

The marker a connoisseur of potholes.

White Jews came here, and Vasco da Gama
The canals swell with suicides

Brides of empire, of Malabar

The Taj Express

1

Night expresses hooting across India,
The clank and shunt of an empire

Outstaying its welcome. I open eyes
To an ayah's eyes, the shuffle of cards.

Coaldust on my tongue like a wafer,
And in a swaying lavatory a woman's

Knees slanting moonlight at her belly.
The engines hiss and spill.

The Deccan moored to huge mango trees,
Mosquito nets like child brides.

Stations are marble dormitories, fruitstalls
Inset like altars, wax dripping—

An air of the morgue, all these sleepers
Huddled like mailbags without addresses.

Dawn of papaya and fresh lime.

2

The burra-sahib dressed as for the golfcourse,
Shorts, suede shoes, sports shirt open at the neck.

Outside, the bearer chews *pan* and betel,
Mouth smeared on the edge of haemorrhage.

Whisky and crime stories, and at halts wreaths
Of tuberoses and marigold, ash ceremonies.

Bottles in a dressing case gaudy as spices
In Bow Bazaar, crushed essences like shut parasols.

The rattle of points and bangles. The air
Is sulphurous, spiralling out of mutiny,

The embrace of miners and goddesses,
Where everything escapes, hands palm upward.

Part IV

Before Racing

Pink layer of icing sugar,
Till the straw sun dissolves it,
And the Downs, drained by the cold
Of their green, sweep grey
To grey sea. Trees are mastheads.

Elements of blue like eyelids
Open sky clinking iron
With hooves of horses on bridle
Paths, back after riding out,
And the lanes lathered with breath.

As yet it is anybody's
Morning, a slate clouded
With nothing; but gradually,
Under the cold, something's
Moving, beginning to conspire
Towards a finish flushed with silver.

Driving to Fontwell

Scoops of mist in hills that swing
And feint away seaward, tweed smudges
Through windscreen wipers, the season
Turning as the Citröen turns to tilt
The mercury of the river, boats
Tethered like horses, horses still as boats.
We pass horseboxes, bookmakers equipped like fishermen,
Shopkeepers in a small way of business
Hurrying through autumn as if it were escaping them.

And a ticket falls from my raincoat
Hidroplanador Macau Para Hongkong
The same kind of day, islands
Shrinking in mist, the South China sea
The colour of the Adur, junks
Scattered like bits of brown leaf,
Paddleboats of the Companhia de Navegaçao Shun Tak
Noisy with whores and booze and music,
Smells of urine and shrimps,
That particular sweat exuded by gamblers.

The old *Taipa* went down,
Turning turtle in a typhoon, and I can smell
The same racecourse sweat now, smoke clearing
To faces yellow over green baize,
As looking from Lukinachow over the frontier
To Red China, fishermen and guards
Patrolling the Shumchun river, the mist
Came up at one, like off the Adur,
Gelatinous, and set in it
Tethered boats, horses, portraits of Mao.

Cross-talk to a Psychiatric Hospital

1
The phone rings and I know it's you,
But not exactly who—a dull
And dopy voice with flat sedated lull
Between the static; or inconsequential blonde
Whose tales of orgy, drink or fond
Pursuit of that oblivion just beyond
Belief are rich in misses
Too close for comfort or consoling kisses?

2
I hear the crackling air alive
With those invading eyes your guilt contrives
And wonder which of two, who both
Are on the line today and seeming loth
To let the other speak, will say goodbye,
Penitent or punitive. And when I ask—
Not able to look you in the eye,
But taking your fantasies to task—
Whether you believe a word you say, you reply
Dutifully, no I believe nothing at all,
Suddenly bereft, letting the receiver fall.

3
I wait across a county like a hull
Low down in water, rain a dripping sail,
Then put the specious arguments on view
To make the ward, its wretched crew,
Fade into oblivion. But they'll come back
When I ring off, re-forming for attack,
And then we'll have the same old cycle,
Despair, revenge, the familiar trickle
Of blood or almost overdose. A kind of game,
Only the stakes are villainous and your name
Still fragile: unless you mean to lose
The body and the talent too promising to use.

Return to Wilhelmshaven

Field-grey of ghost officers, of survivors,
Black leather in coats swung like opera
Full length with menace, black boots,
Black gauntlets in puffs of dust
Down country lanes, eagles, goggles,
Eyeglasses, iron-crosses, and labourers
With clanking milkchurns and the blank
Surprised look of scarecrows.
After so many years
The country seems curiously tame
And lobotomized, the old
Merely old, the pinewoods cut, lakes dredged.

Recognition has gone out of the eyes
That have become glass, sightless.
They cannot remember the barracks
Nights of conquest, sinkings, song,
A creeper of fog making
Your own memory seem faulty,
Men in white coats with syringes
Taking the pain from futility,
Obliterating the old barracks the old days.

Sailors off duty whistling after girls
In the long evenings corn becoming sea-blue
Milk blondes with milk-blue eyes
I remember the obstinacy
Of spires against gales of watered ice,
Land flattened by protestantism
Hovering like a smell of old vegetables,
Heine and Heineken, brass bands
And a dog with three legs,
Cyclists with coats open like men
Exposing themselves and nothing to expose.

The landmarks have been bulldozed
Signposts point the wrong way
In housing estates cows are marooned
It is hard to put much face
To so depressing a past, the mirrors
Of lakes empty of embellishment
Friesian girls with legs in black silk
Friesian ports with men on one leg.

Bathing huts line the old quays,
Postcards of U-boats and holidaymakers
In striped costumes—the Kaiser
And blue movies—what remains constant
Are the headstones like fields of green teeth
Shingle and sea flapping like tarpaulins
The land running out running down.

Murmansk

The snow whisper of bows through water
Asking and answer in their lift
And screw, ceremonials
Of salt and savagery,
Burial of man and mermaid.

On those last ski slopes
Voices still murmur
Ciels de Murmansk, ceilings, sea-eels,
Water-skiers with lovely backs
Arched before breaking.

I remember the thirst of Murmansk
The great eyelids of water.
Can one ever see through them?

U-Boat in the Arctic

From seas that had been dull
For days, white horses like real
White horses with startled eyes grew
Out of troughs and with slew
And heave of flanks like seal
Or whale the slack liquorice hull
Of a U-boat surfacing. Then
It becomes merely a matter when,
And through the angled periscope who.

Yearlings

A string of horses black against the snow,
The December light already beginning to go

And the beeches absorbing them, a rust
Tunnel through which like mist

They jog, shadowy invaders.
Caparisoned, they suggest courtliness

And lineage, heirs
To historic names whose sires

Gaze through hooded eyes,
Still innocent of pride or surprise.

Donkeys at Dusk

All day they had stood in the heat
Like statues, immune to weather
Or flies, but occasionally towing
Plaster effigies to new moorings.

Then, in the cool,
Powdery bodies striped with sunset,
They seemed to lose patience,
Charging like zebra for water.
And, as suddenly, stopped,
Atavism gone out of them,
But the stream returning their manes,
Clouds racing to dispersal.

Gandhi on the Rhine

The indigo glint of this river,
Bones of Prussian thoroughbreds crushed
To make so pure a blue

And the glint of this Indian
Immobile behind perfectly round glasses
Hooked over huge queries.

I see Gandhi bending over me
A lamp like a halo
And the round walnut skull with huge ears
The glint of his specs in mid-air
Humming like wires

And that day in his museum
Traffic melting in the heat
The case with his specs
And sandals, the assassin's bullet
Like an old filling

Cut-out photographs
With grins curling at the edges
Dead marigolds on black marble
The sickly resonance of hysteria

The glint of this river
Is the glint carried all these years
By Gandhi's glasses bent over me,
The perfectly round glasses of this Indian.

Bangkok Massage Parlour

He notices the tightness of her buttocks
As she walks his spine in white socks,
The thighs dough-coloured up to blue shorts.
Her customers, she begins, are all sorts,
Cracking his fingers and toes,
But mostly Vietnam G.I. Joes
On R and R, and in the monsoons
Her husband squirts her with a hose,
Sometimes his eyes smoky as he croons
Sinatra, thrashing her spread buttocks.
She kneads his shoulders and neck,
In her choked giggle complaining what a wreck
He makes her and how limp his long cock,
Prices still going up in the floating market,
The commies being shot, and it's always wet
Living on a Klong, while her friend there
Near the temple of Wat Arun can usually share
A taxi being on the tourist beat, and she rubs
Coconut oil on his belly and her bubs
Brush his chest, like oxygen masks
So rubbery and inflatable, and she asks
If he'd like an outing on the Chao Phya river
On Sunday with a friend, is that the liver?,
They could go to Thai boxing or the races.
And he thought there's always some blemish,
Myopia, or bandy legs, or pockmarks on their faces,
Sad when their hair is marvellously black
And thick, and their bodies as slippery as fish
In the steam, and their minds so one-track.

Autumn in Hamburg

Two nights running in the early hours
I've woken to imagine their footsteps
Echo past the Jungfernstieg. They round
The Alster like black scarecrows flapping arms,
The woman with such puffy eyes
The man in homburg and smoked glasses.

They seemed to swivel with ugly shoos and laughs,
Herding me off the pavement like an animal
Into the traffic. Once vaguely pretty
In languid southern fashion, she smells
Of scent and doughnut, smiles black ice.
His coat is fur-lined, reaching to his calves.

It's hard to reconcile their malice,
Or did I witness once, in squalor,
Their nightly scavenging for rations,
The dustbin trips, like werewolves on the prowl?
Or meet him in his palmy days
A Commandant's corset on his banker's body,
The double-lightning on the turkey collar?

A Death in the Woods

She lay naked in the back seat,
Legs tucked up, knees to her breasts,
The black between the loosened buttocks
A slit fur in soft white.
Remembering gundogs, wetness, stopped clocks,
He digs, stamping down leaves, rests.
The windows become opaque and the heat
Has made the small hairs stick
To her body as if painted. The light
Is cold moonlight and her eyes
Once clouds smoky with semen pop
Like green grapes. Birds drop
From thin branches, and the smell
Of gunshot drifts like mist, gunpowder
Blue over nothingness and the noise louder
In his head, dragging her by the thighs.
He can't lose her, nor hear the click.
A second shot. He's done the job well.

Part V

Sussex Portraits

A Cricketer in Retirement

For George Cox

The marine and the regency, sea frets,
And somewhere the Downs backing a station
Like a Victorian conservatory. I come upon
A scorecard yellow as old flannels and suddenly
I see him, smilingly prowling the covers
In soft shoes, shirt rolled to the forearm,
Light as a yacht swaying at its moorings,
But socially dangerous. An element
Of silk, of ease, with none of the old dutiful
Sense of the regiment, the parade-ground
Posture that gave even the best of them the air of retainers.
Instead, a kind of compassion linking top hats
With turnips, the traditional turning to devilry.
One apart, yet part all the same,
Of that familiar pattern of families,
Parkses and Langridges, Tates and Oakes and Gilligans,
Griffiths and Busses, Sussex is rich in,
The soft air phrased by their fickleness.

Never one for half-measures, as generous
With ducks as half-centuries, he seemed
To calculate extravagance, waywardly spendthrift
With the cold calculators, Yorkshire, the Australians,
Hove and the Saffrons ablaze with his fireworks,
Dad wincing in his grave. With others,
Less challenging, he was often vulnerable,
Giving his wicket to those who were glad of it,
Indulgently negligent against parachuting spinners.
Now there are no scorecards, just pulled hamstrings
In village cricket and instead of fancy-free

Strokes in festival arenas the soothing
Of successors. The forearms make gardens,
And the journeys have lengthened, a sunset
Of orchards and vineyards, where reclining in a bath
Of imperial proportions he observes a wife
As delicate with pastry as he was at the wicket.

Death of a Trainer

In Memory of Alan Oughton

Among fellow jockeys bandy and small
He was straight as a board and tall,
So long to the knees
He could pick up and squeeze
Novices and old rogues round all sorts of courses.
Neither bred to the sea nor horses,
The son of a Pompey tailor,
He walked with brisk roll of a sailor,
Tilted, as by saddle or quarter deck,
A curve from hipbone to neck.

Falls caught up with him, of the kind habitual
To riders over sticks, but he seemed at last
Safe in his Findon stables, at his disposal
A handful of jumpers not especially fast
Nor clever, but amenable to discipline
And patience, ridden out on a skyline
Of downland and sea, in lime dawn
Or half darkness, clouds torn
By gales blistering the channel,
Mist thickening beechwoods to flannel.

Busy as a ship, smelling of hay
And leather, of mash and linseed,
The yard seemed that ideal harbour
In which work has the essence of play,
Day-long, night-long, obedient to need,
The summer's sweetness, winter's bleak labour.
But season following season, winner
Following winner, so did pain circle,
Eyes grow strained and the thin body thinner,
Until there was only the long hell.

What I still see is a skeletal guy
Half imagined, half real, between races at Fontwell,
Saddle under one arm, threading his way
Through the weighing room, or wiping jellied eel
From his lips, sawdust running out of him
As he drops in the distance, each limb
Jerky as if on a string, patch
Over one eye, trilby dead straight,
And a gelding quickening to snatch
Up the verdict, just leaving it too late.

Mary Stephens, R.I.P.

Impossible not to picture you still
As the below-stairs skivvy, all frill
And fancy in mob-cap and apron,
A childhood on all fours on iron-
Hard floors, scouring pans, peeling
Potatoes, whatever had to be done kneeling,
So your joints became as rounded as onions.
But whatever you put your hand to,
Swearing like a trooper, true blue,
Had the hallmark of your personal
Attention, Embassy party, Hunt Ball,
Whatever unpredictable Servants' Hall
You landed up in, Londonderry
Or Dublin, fresh as a berry
And with that same fine finish
You gave to whatever dish
Or silver took your fancy to cherish.

You remained irretrievably Irish, though fifty
Years had passed since you came to Dublin
From the West, head full of Original Sin,
And it was most of a life later before
We got the benefit of your skills
In the kitchen, your temper and thrifty
Ways, entering the back door
Like a tinker with a caravan of ills
And a tom on a string, our hearts
At the same time. Commodore of roasts
And soufflés, mistress of soups and tarts,
You treated the kitchen like a bridge,
Able Seaman tied to the table, the edge
Of your tongue ready for whoever went past
When you felt in the mood for a barney,
Though the outbursts were brief, and not many.

How the parlour maid became such a genius
Is an aspect of magic, like the metamorphosis
From spinster to kind of unmarried duchess.

Then, one fine day, you suddenly had enough
Of the bloody Aga, fumes, bending, the lot,
And we bundled you off with your stuff
And the cat to a seaside flat
Not too far off, but where he peed
All over the neighbours' plants and got
A full chamber on his head for his pains,
And you vowed blue murder if it happened again,
Though alas there was no need.
Dear Mary, you hadn't a good word
For too many, but you were good
In the way few ever are,
With a natural distinction, the ability
To separate sheep from the goats
At a glance, or allow a rare note
Of approval—dear Mary, pity

Was not something you ever asked for,
Even when your journeys to hospital and back
Had become increasingly pointless, the war
Intensifying over the cat, and the lack
Of good neighbours made worse by your bark,
And it was probably we more than you
Who mourned over air gone suddenly slack,
Your bloomers like sails on a sagging line,
The cat in the area biding its time,
One less with whom to love and wrangle,
Waves clawing their way up winter shingle,
And your face going down for the final time,
Mob cap, stone floors, Holy Mother, green coastline. . . .

In Memory of Fred Codling

An element of freefall about the roses
You planted ten years ago, staking them
To pear trees and apple, so that now
They float in the orchard like pink parachutes,
Precariously perched, as if a faint wind
Would up-end them. But they're more solid
Than that in their attachment, as you were
To this garden, going about your business
With Norfolk gruffness, glad to be alien
In such soft contours, incurably resistant.

And watching without you your roses
Climb to new heights I regret that so often
You were solitary, even more than you wanted,
Nursing your grievances, that real closeness
Only came with your illness, plans
For new plantings, a trout pond
To alleviate retirement, already mirages
Neither believed in. Now I recall
In this Indian summer your morphia autumn,
The nurse whose face like a tennis racket
You described with sly grin, the last
Delirium when, a Boy again, you clutched
Your discharge from *Warspite*, or imagined yourself
Becalmed on the long voyages to Sydney,
Among flyingfish and dolphins, your eyes
As wide and blue as the Indian ocean.